WORDSOUNDS
AND SIGHTLINES

D0764668

MICHAEL HOROVITZ

Wordsounds
and Sightlines

New & Selected Poems

NEW DEPARTURES

First published in Great Britain 1994
by Sinclair-Stevenson

Reprinted 1994

New edition published as New Departures
#31 by New Departures in 2001
PO Box 9819, London, W11 2GQ, England, U.K.

Copyright © 1994 Michael Horovitz
The author has asserted his moral rights

A CIP catalogue record for this book
is available at the British Library
ISBN 0 902689 20 7

Photoset by Deltatype Limited, Ellesmere Port, South Wirral
Printed and bound in Great Britain
by Bookmarque Ltd, Croydon, Surrey

for Rosi, Adam, and Inge
and, in loving memory
for Frances Horovitz

Contents

Notes and Acknowledgements

I've put this book together as a companion volume and sequel to *Growing Up: Selected Poems & Pictures 1951–1979*.

The poems in the first three sections were written in the 1960s and 1970s, excepting 'for Bernard Stone' (1994), 'Gothic Evanescence' (1982), 'AUBADE' (1985), 'SEA SONG' (1987), 'from The Journal of a Lovesick Parrot' (1980) and 'Gnarling Song' (1990).

The poems in sections IV, V and VI, apart from 'A Fanfare for Thribb' (1978), 'A POSTCARD FROM IRELAND' (1966), 'for Modern Man' (1964), '– How then/– zen Cage' (1964), and 'A Contemplation' (1976), emerged in the 1980s and early 1990s.

'A POSTCARD FROM IRELAND' also exists as an 8′ × 4′ example of 'Paintry', which was reproduced on the cover of the catalogue to my exhibition of 'Bop Paintings, Collages and Picture-Poems' at Jane England's west London gallery in April 1989, and this version was also published in the form of an actual postcard by England & Co.

The idea of the revisitations to poetic places in section IV was initiated by Val Hennessy, who also suggested and helped revise a number of details and phrases in these five poems.

'Fugue for John Cage' was written at Peter Gabriel's 1992 WOMAD recording week, to be spoken with the composer Simon Jeffes's fugal elegy 'for found musicians', based on the sequence of notes C A G E – D E A D (see 'Renaissance man of our time', *Spectator*, 12 September 1992).

The poems have not appeared in my previous volumes, but many of them have been published in anthologies, magazines and newsprint, and broadcast in various media around Britain, Europe and North America. Several were read, performed or sung on 'Alive and Kicking' (Adrian Mitchell and Ann Wolf's ITV series); on 'Late Night Line-Up' (with Joan Bakewell, BBC2); in John McGrath's BBC TV film 'Mo'; in Gavin Millar's BBC TV film 'Transport by Underground'; and in 'Wholly Communion' (Peter Whitehead's film of the first International Poetry Incarnation at the Royal Albert Hall, London, in 1965). 'Notting Hill Carnival Poem' was included on the first *Poetry Olympics* compilation LP.

Some of the poems were read on 'Night Ride' presented by John Peel on BBC Radio 1, 'Midweek' with Ned Sherrin on BBC Radio 4, and on the following BBC Radio 3 programmes: 'Anglo-Jewish Poetry' presented by John Kershaw; 'Mixing It' presented by Robert Sandall and Mark Russell; and 'A New Sound – British Beat Poetry', 'Poetry Now', and transcripts from the two Royal Albert Hall readings of 1965 and 1966, all edited and presented by the late lamented George MacBeth.

Some of the poems have appeared in the following anthologies: the Arts Council's *New Poetry 6*, ed. Ted Hughes; *The Blue Nose Poetry Anthology,* ed. Martyn Crucefix et al; *Book 'im: A Tribute to Bernard Stone,* ed. Barry Miles; *Children of Albion,* ed. Michael Horovitz; *C'mon Everybody: Poetry of the Dance,* ed. Pete Morgan; *An Enitharmon Anthology for Alan Clodd,* ed. Stephen Stuart-Smith; *Life doesn't frighten me at all*, ed. John Agard; *The New British Poetry,* ed. Dave Cunliffe and Tina Morris; *Making Love: the Picador Book of Erotic Verse,* ed. Alan Bold; *New Sounds in British Poetry,* ed. Anselm Hollo; *New Writing & Writers 15,* ed. John Calder; *PEN New Poetry 1,* ed. Robert Nye; *PEN New Poetry 2,* ed. Elaine Feinstein; *Poems for Alan Hancox,* ed. Alan Tucker; *The Poetry Book Society Anthology 1988–1989* ed. David Constantine; *Nineties Poetry,* ed. Graham Ackroyd; *Survivors' Anthology 2,* ed. Jenny Ford et al; *Transformation: the Poetry of Spiritual Consciousness*, ed. Jay Ramsay; *Wholly Communion,* ed. Peter Whitehead.

Some of the poems have also appeared in the following magazines: *Agenda, Angel Exhaust; Arc; Bananas; Black Eggs; City Lights Journal; City Limits; De Tafel Ronde; Evergreen; Gargoyle; Global Tapestry; Haiku* (Wolverhampton); *ICA Bulletin; Jewish Chronicle; Kulchur; Labris; Live New Departures* programmes; *New Departures; New Statesman & Society; New York Quarterly; Ostinato; Other Poetry; Oz; Paperway; Phantomas; Poetmeat; Poetry Review; Resurgence; Rhinozeros; The Rialto; Sandwiches; Spectator; Splitter; Streetword; Stride; Törn; Tlaloc; Transatlantic Review; Ver Sacrum; Words International.*

Many thanks to the producers, editors and publishers of all these, and also of any other media that have communicated any of these poems, but have been inadvertently omitted here.

Special thanks also to Susie Allfrey, Inge Elsa Laird, Rachel Peddie, David Russell and Neil Taylor, for their invaluable help.

I InterCity Poems

InterCity Animal

. . . Had to run
hard to catch this train
– Hoarse sensation
from belly to brain
shuddering, juddering
the sou'westerly rain
                              express
stutters to halt amid ploughed
fields – easier to
write now, *hee-haws and
hoots*, I shift to lean
more easily, so do
neighbours – though city-bound
gent strides
                    out of our compartment
and pulls down window
– This compartment all aware
of me scribbling now
suddenly urgent
with electric energy from
another train that whizzes past
    . . . *whoosh*: abrupt silence
– Footsteps pass . . . down
the corridor – *Cotswold Life*
shiny journal crackles,
embarrassed country girl
scratches at stocking, per-
functory conversation resumes as
train starts up I stop

Between Stops

Long windowseats ease us out
of the jumbled foyer,
jostling city
scaffoldings and escarpments
give way to more detached landscapes
as faster
yet still sedately, frame by frame
this afternoon's movie
opens in earnest:
friendly Mr Guard
voices over the credits
and we settle back
secure at last in contemplation
of the master-planned time-and-motion
study we booked for. Fields and woods
flash up, scuffed by wind, whilst
clouds overtaken continue probing
the broad sky's canvas
with Van Goghy brush strokes, seeming
almost to swash the stubble – to
passengers bent on imbibing
the stippled newsprint type
marks of man. Horses huddled
grazing near ponds
alter the focus, crows and seagulls
flap and wheel
their respective difference (and
distance) of quests
from our own creature comforts, 'lost
in thoughts' . . . . . till
– *Tickets please*, snap out of it – back to
the workaday train slows down, you
look up, and a
BIG house sails into view
smoking three, four – numberless cars,

4

private lake gleaming with speedboats,
roasting-sheep, rock-bands in the patio
– the whole Dolce Vita-in-the-country bit
esplanades away from the passing
High Speed electrified bird's eye instamatic freeze

Ladbroke Grove . . .

Rain.   Parked vans, gutters
Swarming with leaves
Gleaming in Ladbroke Grove
Rain.   Inside
Budgies beep, inside
Their cage, inside
The flat – which houses also
People – asleep, innocently
Or not, till –
Soon, self-alarmed, they
Clock in
To rage, routine, old age: fleeting
Pleasures, much pain, the same
As elsewhere across London, in
Ladbroke Grove
Rain; but deep
                down
                      inside
A few of those cages, rain
       does not
     stop
   play –

Notting Hill Carnival Poem*

A pageant of floating foliage
beating conga drums and dustbin lids
with clarion pipes and wild smoke paint
and fancy dress stirs joy
enough to get
                    policemen even dancing
up the Grove – *O rittum*, the rhythm
joins peaceloving light-
and dark-skinned hands
and hearts and heads and bands
                    in jumping jubilee –
grabbing great branches, a shuffling swaying
triumphal march in glad hurrah – *every-*
body do dis t'ing
– children – all ages
chorusing – 'We all live
                    in a *yell*ow submarine'
– trumpeting tin bam good-time stomp –
a sun-smiling wide-open steelpan-chromatic
neighbourhood party making love not war
– and the televisions all around
          have closed their electronic eyes
                    knocked out by spontaneous reality
      now autumn welcomes you to spring
in Notting Hill,
                    where universe collides
      with universe, and still
          nothing gets broken

---

* This was written at the first Notting Hill Carnival in August 1966, which was
a relatively small-scale revival of the pre-war Notting Hill Fayre, set up by a
multiracial group of community-minded local residents; essentially it was just
a summer festival street-party. Over the years the event has tended to get
aggrandised, congested, over-amplified, and sometimes spoiled by a tiny
fraction of nasties, or by the conflicting vested interests of non-celebrants.
Nevertheless: '. . . *Lawd, don' stop the Carnival!*'

Spring Welcomes You to London

— the poster sings and a merry
engine washes the Soho streets
No dragons no nets it's good
to be up and about — till
This man 7 a.m. Sunday sunshine
cowering on the Astoria steps
grabs three pigeons (deaf
to their agitated cooing) stashed
in his plush red shooting-brake
— What, I shout before he can slam the doors
What are you taking the pigeons away?
— *Whadd'ya mean what am I taking the pigeons away?*
What's it look like I'm doin'?   — But why?
They've as much right as you to roam the city
— and they're pretty —   *Pretty? ?*
That's what you think isit ya gett —
Looga' that: they Shit allover the place
No hygiene . . . What we call
Trafalgar Square's buried under their droppins —
They use the roads as airways
An' dive under the cars —
And the more on'em there are
The more they reproduce their 'orrible selves
— There's bye-laws bein' passed . . .   And in chimes
a hatchet-faced policeman loomed abreast:
They pick the silver tops offof milkbottles
for 'ippies to drain an' smash —
   Shit, I say to myself, What   — but behind our backs
a tiny wizened cleaningwoman's pissing herself
with laughter — the birds flapped up the basket-lid
and out after breadcrumbs she's sprinkled
there on the open street they dodge the traffic
a busy crooning throng of doves pigeons robins sparrows —
Multinous fowl breakfasting at her behest then

shimmering up the treetop green of Golden Square
delivered by wings from civic petty fogs
and the lurking scraowlcats to boot –

Soho Awakening

for Stan Tracey

mind's eye opens afresh
from dreamgleam trance

in a pool of petrol
all tones dance

crescent   city   moon
incandescent   through vapours
cuts   back to the arc
of historic   time

sun's spectrum swells
in park enclaves
rainbows plash
off ducks back waters

piercing skylight and airshaft
through these salvage dumped streets
and bird-brimming squares

even glances down
the underground

Amsterdam

Dinky clocks peal
Musical hours, witness
Haiku shock inklings

& cocks in the head
Of the big frog ego

Drowned by each glaring
Small pond flash –

Yellow leaves
    as they quit
        each tree –
To hit
    the moonlit
        canal-skin

Leaving ripples that line
Mental traveller's brow

    – Till splitting

New York

without wheels
– swayed and rocked
dizzy – 'off my feet'

by the endless
procession of wheels

– roiling around
nether depths
of a canyon
from which to rise again

atop

the thin
vertical
columns
– out to
limitless
light . . .

– *rats!*
It's a long
hard
climb
to the bliss of
them
thar
hills

New York!

New York!

. . . City
of gigantic
matchbox
tentacles

– I'm frightened

the clothes
horse
scaffoldings
up there

will fall
and tromp
my head

with their vast
milliard

street-fighting

hooves –

'DANGER – MEN AT WORK'

('*You can't help falling for a Walls*'
– Ice-cream advertising jingle, mid-1960s)

Collages of humanity we may be
maimed by governments elect
   for arms arms arms
but one thing's for sure:

ARMY   SURPLUS

– as announced by worldwide stores
ever since the last three wars

along with:

LAST THREE DAYS – !
EVERYTHING   *MUST*   GO!

   – NEWS OF THE WORLD?

Closed for Mars –

'All Human Life is there'

(the rats race like people)

Making it
corrodes
like hard-
coloured rock
through and through
– you can eat
rock
but the market
eats
you –

Dangermen at work
charging the earth

The price remains long after
the value is forgotten —

                              'eat well — *eat Walls!*'
                                — and shit bricks —

                              if you take in every-
                                    thing they say
                              You can't help falling —

  God's in his Heaven
      Creating Earth

    When he gets down here
        He's going to raise

                        Hell.

in Paris

. . . arise at dawn from
foam rubber blue pillow
pink blanket piss flush
brush teeth – miss the feel
of rush mats underfoot as
in London – but never mind
that – I may be a Londoner
but this is Paris – down the
stairs jumping 3-at-a-time
out to the forecourt – 'Good-
Day *Sun*shine' – ask young girls –
student couples – restaurateurs
opening their doors for breakfast
– for directions – fart belch
buy croissant & apple turnover –
munch in streets ('a small turnover') – read messages on walls
wind way through streets wide &
narrow – just noticing mosaic
of cobbles on streets – historic
architectures of church & lion's
mouths & classic statues –
bleach & iron smocked nuns in
convent vestibules – flamboyant
sexy walks of Paris business-ladies
lines from the past – '*A l'ombre*
des arbres et jeunes filles' –
fall on grass in Luxembourg
Gardens tall trees & voices
in them laugh & rustle
their skirts & leaves
– so young – so green
'*Les lauriers sont coupés*'

16

– the garden of love
open & seen – flowers toss
their heads in the breeze
– young lovers swing
their hips – I sneeze
for the earth is full
of sky today – & the sky
replete with sun – & birds
quietly jingling – their beaks
still snatching the
last shreds of night
plying darker lines of melody
across the dazzling noonday light . . .

II Light Verse

LIGHT MOTIFS

(Sequence of themes for chanting
& possible counterpoint with music
or birdsong or other sounds; several
voices could repeat 'light' & other phrases in tonal,
melodic, rhythmic variation)

1

Light   blazes white
              early

Light   sounds the night
              cascading

Light   black
              into white

              changing
              key
              note
              upon round
              mid
                  note

Light   tinkling shells
              spells

              – white
              and black
              skinless
Light

2

Light bulb
    splits
    at sun's start

    there   where
    light clouds
    passed over

    white moon
    shining full
    on night's haven

    cream white
    milky way
    trickling
             – Light

3

Light breeze
Daylight ease
Alights
Through trees

On light
Without fire
Smoke
Without cloud
Of plight
Or fright

– Light of mind
– Bright breath
– Kiss of light!

4

Enlightenment

is
sometimes

breathing

the street lamp

out

at dawn

and reading

between

the branches

a map
of sky

space –

pure light

5

Till	till –
Till	later

'*More* Light'
– Wanting lighter
The Word
Weighed Heavy

And Light		begat Blight
– Then was Light		wanted Fight
And diminished	in anguish	for Might

– Then dragon
Spat fire
Heavens trembled
Desire
In anger
Walls shook

Hearths shuddered

And darkness
Closed the book

6

But soft   – next
Day's eye
Throws up
New sight
– Opens – senses
Again

– Poet sings
O Pen!

Opens fire
– Opens head:
O pen – O pen –   Open

– Book
        of Life!

When God said
There was light
There was so
Much light
The rumour went
You could see
For miles –

7

Thunder claps –
Lightning strikes
At the heart
Of man

– Of *a* man
– *This* man

And this word
Was wed:

'– Win bread'!

– Till unlocked
From the heart
And light-
Loving head
– Bedrock said:

> light sleeping
>
> – wife shining
>
> light stirring
>
> – wife waning
>
> wife sleeping
>
> light shining
>
> – wife waking

Night light shining

Light wife twining

> – Till

Baby waking!

Baby crying

– Light flying

    . . . Mind

    resting

– Baby shining

– Wife shining

    (not)

    minding

– Light

        8

Moon pales
at sun's lustre

Moon flight
at bird light

Till morning calls give way
to the bright noonday

In heat
Light of heat
We begin

– Out of the dark
We came

Into the dark
We'll go

Travelling

And still

Life

– In clouds
– In height
– In shade

– In light.

Intimations of Mortality

Farmer said to the bo'-weevil
'You've gotta get off my land'
— Bo'-weevil said to the farmer
'You sound just like a man . . .'
Leadbelly, *Looking for a Home*

Have Not – will try

Have lots . . . . . . will tie

  . . . Own house
  – Kill mouse

        . . . What mouse
        – cheese mouse

  – All mice
  are cheese mice

. . . All cheese
is mouse cheese

       – as for holes –
       all holes
       are mouseholes

  . . . and all mice
  are hole mice

. . . . . . This could
go on
    for ever

. . . . . . This should
never
    have begun

    . . . . . . considering

    how

```
      – cheese
         – chalk
            – flowers
   – pork
   . . . . . . life
   . . . all
            over
                  so
                     very
                        soon –
```

After Browning

Summer's done –
Birds in their heaven

– All's well with the worm.

On the Road Again

(After Neal Cassady, Kerouac et al)

– Nothing left
at all . . .

                              – Not a goddamned thing
                              right . . .

          . . . *FULL SPEED AHEAD!*

Smoke
less//
Inter
zone

(Written after the 14-hour Technicolor Dream
at Alexandra Palace, London, April 1967)

— After another
Allnite rave
Envisioning
Mine owne
   stomping micromatic macromantric psycho-
                             Chassidelique pop-troupe
— 'The Negative
Capabilities'! —
   yawping chanting droning whooping recharging the
     earth's
   Afro-American Asiaticking over Jeru
                        salemic Huzza grailzapp
                        v i b r a t i o n s
— I had to go
        & buy
             the 3 posh Sunday papers —
Shat & vomited into them
             all the phantastic food & drink
             & orgiasmic sax-candied groove-juice
             gorged down my gullet
             over the previous 36 hours
— rolled it into an immense
but not to me at all grotesque
multi-
     techni-
         colour-
             supplemented
                   joint
& was just about to light it
   When my wife comes round the corner
   and says   Hey wait
   I want to read that —

for Bernard Stone at 70

For thirty years now your Aladdin's caves of making
Have kept countless Parnassian souls their thirsts a-slaking.
   The first Turret Bookshop in Kensington's Church Walk
Was the merriest backwater of that time,
                                where writers went to talk
And browse, carouse and mingle at perpetual Sabbath, wet or fine
   For the limitless friendship, peanuts, wine
Dispensed by you, Herr Stein – and every year thereafter
You've gone on topping us up with lightsome gossip and laughter.
   Each of your emporia has functioned as oasis
Athwart the oft-so-barren deserts of Lundane literary paces:
   The sanguine hospitality of Chaucer's frolicky Franklin
Conspires with mischief, wit and cunning, a flash of Chaplin
And your Puckish joy at people's infinite varieties,
To strip the transactions you host of all their customary pieties
   – And though the timeless Bohemian air
                          that permeates your Turrets
Is shared by a rare few stores affording respite
To literati in Paris, New York and California,
   No place in Albion comes near to being hornier
Than yours at stirring up whole plethora of excitations,
Introductions, collaborations, publications, declamations,
Affrays and affairs of hearts and heads and bodies,
Smiles of summer nights, huge winter toddies
   Encouraging the young, unknown, neglected, old
And justly famed, unjustly scorned, hard-sold
Or remaindered . . . grateful beneficiaries alike
Of your largesse – enabler, blithe custodian of the sacred book
Of life
   – but soft: here's wishing you, ere I wax seriously soupy
– A zillion happy returns, umpteen yonks more
                      of Making Whoopee!

'Making Whoopee' is Mr Stone's favourite song.

HOT WINE

(incantatory recipe)

for Cornelius Cardew

now now
        then then
enough of your sauce –
        pan – no
broiling and bubbling –
        if you boil it
you spoil it –
    now – fling nutmeg in
plap – tip in zest
        of orange peels –
taste taste – then add
        one half teaspoon
of sugar – *really really* –
        does it *really* taste
better this way –
        i can touch – cloves
i can say – *Cheers* –
        i can smell – cinnamon
i can hear – simmering
        jazz of Young – Christian
Monk – Getz –

        Dizzy –   *Shazam!*

Go Go Go . . . . . .

        i can see . . . double –

i can get . . . dizzy

        and still stay cool –

i can i can i can –

        and what if I can't –

i can drink . . . . . .

        hot wine –

                                        gets –   gets –
gets you – gets you –

                              gets you cooler –   if you
if you – leave it till –

                                        later –   it's safer –
safer

to cool it

        cool it –

                        in a stainless
                                        steel
                                                        saucepan
that gives the wine
                        a chance –
                                to get warm
                                        and stay cool
in the first place –
                        the
                                first
                                        place
                                                – coolest
                                                        – and so
and so
        on –
                and
                        soon –
                                cool
                                wine
                                        is
                                                hot
                                                        wine
        is

                – drunk

                                – like

                                . . . *you!*

                                35

The Lady G Rides Again

They said the young lady-god Ivor
in her lust to become a famed diva
rode a cock horse with no clothes on
and trampled the dean of the Sorbonne

'Nonsense your honours' she cried
'The horse that I rode on was slipshod'

'Strike that from the record'
Our Father-god ruled –
' 'Twas a footling slip of the tongue'

'Stuff that' she tootled, really annoyed
'That slip was paid for by Sigmund Freud'

'I always knew that shrink was an odd bod'
said an old-god, eager to get her stung –
'But I didn't know he was such a generous blacksmith'

'He sometimes went by the name of Smith,
But he wasn't black & that's the truth' –
She swore, & rested her case
on the wig of the judge, who lost his place

& sat stunned in his seat whilst she beat her retreat
divesting her clothes when her hooves hit the street
for that was her way of being neat
(the most sensible way, in that Coventry heat)

– then divesting the hooves & finding her feet
she danced over the rooves her frech lover to meet
& they shrank singing arias no ant can repeat
– leaving us, & her horse, to suck history's teat.

Gothic Evanescence

(comic-strip poem)

for RDL

What spiked and grisly clanking of chains throughout the night
whose god spills a watering-can of moonbeams
splayed across moats and dungeons crammed brimful
with ruthlessly grated limbs, rotting
coffins of ashes of once young lovers'
cunts cocks balls breasts arses mouldering oblivious . . . to

what slimy inroads of reptilian amours and excrescence,
of vultures –   tarantulas –   pterodactyls
circling . . . closing . . . roiling . . .

whilst savage amplified crow-calls and rook KRRAAAKs
flood chock the ears of a damsel shackled in the bell tower
of this highwalled bayonet-battlemented clifftop garage?

Her tears cascade to rills that well about her sandalled feet
above the ankles now, but her cruel guardians,
the firefanged tank-hooved centaurs, only cackle and screetch
at her discomfiture

                              – till
on sudden, all these sounds and agencies
of torture and encroachment falter, then dissolve
as the heart of darkness fades
beneath a muslin . . . soft furnishings of day
with steady spurts of chirrupy birdage,
delivery vans, good egg –   milkfloats,
cleaners, papers   – the ordinary alarums
of ground control
that monitor, and electricly dismiss
the incipient terrorists called

                              our dreams.

Theatrical Dream 1993

Security alerts and the pile-up
Of traffic jams and detours meant
I only got there with seconds to go
Before the final bell for Curtain Up
– Just as well the wife
Had got there early and picked up
Our promised comps.
                A disapproving usher
Bustled us into rickety chairs
Strewn up a draughty siding on the far right
At the back, from which we couldn't see
A millimetre of the stage. In fact,
Although a few house lights were still aglow,
All we could infer was one another's downcast
Shapes, plus those of six or seven
Fellow prisoners huddled round the alcove,
And – if we looked left – the walkway
Behind the back row of the stalls.

   Frances and the others just sat there
Stiffly, but '– Bollocks to this' I shouted
And (though the play had started) sprang up
Angrily demanding a better view. But
The theatre staff had vanished
Leaving an auditorium seething with unease.

   Pinter, soliloquising centre stage,
Affected to ignore the strident clamour
Of arguments and mounting anarchy
Beneath him. It seemed
Those who'd paid least
Had the best seats, and weren't about
To budge from them.   '– We blew £300 a bum
For the Royal Box,' a blancmange-bosomed
Blue-rinse-dowagery trout

In fur boa, evening dress and pearls
Elocuted from our dank corner:
'What sort of Royal Box
Do you call *this*?' '– Why,' answered Ken
Livingstone's voice chuckling over the Tannoy,
'A *right* royal one of course –'

   Just then a sirening squad of riot police
Stormed jets of fluorescent tear-gas
Down the centre aisle – the men were harnessed
To a laser-powered guillotine on wheels
Which they heaved onto the stage,
From whence Vanessa, Harold, and the rest
Of the actors fled. Our necks winced
And craned, wondering whose heads
Might be in line to roll

   – But when the Chief Policeman stuffed
His upturned helmet full of petrol-soaked Korans
And placed his own head on the block,
Proclaiming himself in thrall
To the Gods of Abraham, Isaac and Madonna,
The audience was gripped, as by a spell
– Discomforts relished now, under the mutual halo
Of first class in-crowd membership,
For we'd been co-opted – on our mettle
To abet the birth of what we sensed
Was going to be acclaimed the first
Truly revolutionary production
In the history of British drama.

Oral Traditions Revisited

(pop poem)

Listening to *Sounds In-
teresting*, on Radio 3,
I discover that
the heavy rock band
Emerson, Lake & Palmer
have recorded
a bouncy rendition
of Aaron Copland's
'Fanfare
for the Common Man'

– Wow!
The tables   are turning
and the turntable
turning
on
        and round
as Chubby Checker sang
about 35 years ago
'– in an' out
an' up 'n' down
we go –
        o – ooh – o
                        Oh – '
. . . Yeah:
Fan fare!

And quick-change flashes
pump out
– Ralph *Waldo* Emerson
– Vero*n*ica Lake
– *Sam*uel Palmer
                        – Hi there!

III Songpoems & Lyrics

A U B A D E

for I E L

For you

      awakening

your smile
on my lips
           smiling back
to where
a tender tongue-kiss
down – inside
our saliva
of dreams conjoined
glistens
then listens
in a snail's path of s sounds

                      to

early birds stirring
– first faltering
then trilling
so serenely
such sibilant
song sketches,
they seem to echo
shy rumours of
hitherandthithering
skeins of first sunlight

                  un-

winding, wafting
like webbed waves
at the walls,
lapping
then dancing
like our tongues
round the bed

43

gently flicker
lighting up
flames of birdbright high
heartburst w x s sounds

                              – sketching
then etching
veins of new air
                  as of angels
casting night from the sky
winging day through each tree
and window and chimney,
ceiling and stair
– dibbling deep dyes of rose
on aethereal gold sheen
melting mists to new green:

like a sainted medieval spirit
winding fresh flowers
through the black death
dawn
       hits
           town

till God's bloodshot eye
rolls higher, wide open –
bathed clean
to shine fiery but twinkling
azure and clear white,
settling heaven's delight
on the dew-dappled dazzle
of new found ground

– breathing again, now
heaving with sound – gathering
word sounds and work sounds –
thrum of wheels, countless
    footfalls, doors opening
       to sun-stippled leaves
          quick with shadows

– now darting
                    now still

like the shadows
 of your hair
   playing light
     on your cheek
just barely re-
  touching
   your shimmering
    smile

on my mouth, on
  these fingers – all
   over my face
    and body

                    so gladly
awakening

            with you.

Mating Call 1

for F H

Let's
    natch
    and p^{i}ng &
        sough through the night
(a l l   t h r o u g h   e v e r y)
         from bough
      to bough
     of our chosen
tree

. . . .

Let's make
    scoobeedoobee
    or what
        ever comes
n u g a t o r i l y
      or
    (if that's
    the wrongword)
let's
       w
  a y
   n   a
      y

    chirrup
       snort, snore, snuffle, etc
n o i s e s   a s   u s u a l l y

. . . .

        & let's

  some
  times
be
g'gig

gl'yes

   let's

   A
L   L w a y s b e —

     g l e e

Ballad of the Black Knight and Lady White

for Alasdair Clayre, who set it to music

(There's only one kind of mixed marriage
   – that between a woman and a man)

Some time like now
in England's green lands
Young folk know how
to shake   – and hold hands

– Jacko Night and Dolly Day
went into the woods to play
Things were fine, how they were glad
until the skyblue sky went bad –

The rain didn't hover
– it shot to soak
Dark clouds burst all over
this bird and her bloke

They make a beeline for the nearest
barn, take off their wet clothes, & 'Dearest'
says Dolly, 'have you got a match?
Let's warm up a bit over this dry patch'

Settled in the corner – her brewing up
Jack thinks 'Coo – what a nice cup
this doll makes; and I'll bet she bakes
some cakes.'   Night's head shakes . . .

In the cool of the eve, they've strolled
back through the wood, and he's bold
enough to pick some fruits. She says 'Oh
Jack man, it's getting late – '   He says 'Go on, blow

that: I want *you*   – to name the date'.   Happy
Dolly says 'Alright mate, let's make it
snappy – I want *all* of you to be my pappy'
– So Night runs rings round to take it

like a man. Now they're devoted for
a life-time span; it's organised – what's more,
they're in line for a baby carriage –
it's a crazy mixed-up swinging marriage.

Coal-black Jack and snow-white Dolly –
everything in the garden's jolly –
Their house is warm, they watch the telly
– fumigate when things get smelly

> This is their story, this is their song
> Now *don't* try to say something's wrong
> – Tell it good, sing it long
> You won't be sorry if you can be strong.

Soliloquy in the Forest

... Hard pressed between the leaves of the soul's black
book, a poor suffering poet conjures the Muse to
relinquish her patronage:

I'm well-dressed Robin
the Hoodest
redbreast –
a bit   – under the crest
'cos I'm plagued all night
by an amorous pest
who comes on   with a raging unquenchable quest
even unto my very nest
with intent to dishonourably unzip
my sleep skin vest

It's obvious
I'll get no rest
until I prevail upon that   blithering
babbling   bluetitted
moon-madding museumpiece of a   – Muse
& uninvited guest
to renounce her foolish dream   of my pillarbox chest
pressed
upon hers (for I am betrothed
to an ex-
tremely well made
Marionbird –
the best!)

'List, twitmus –

'tis no jest:

this union's blessed

by all that's not retrogressed

& cessed.   Move West, distressed

fowl, or get messed about

in any direction you like   lest – in your zest

to attest

your conviction we'd make bosom pals

thou forgetst

I could have you   – arrested

– & bequested

for molesting

by the Sheriff

of Notting-Hill-Gate –

Epitha-lay-me-on

(An Immodest Proposition: may be sung –
to the tune of 'Habañera' in *Carmen*)

Snip my parsley
Bake my bean
Wash my pants –
Be my queen

– Sniff my snout
& Stick my wicket
– I'll expand your grout
& Fill your bucket

– Nip your cherry
Bite your bud,
Churn our milk
To cheesy mud

– Spill your beans
& Spring your trap,
Swill your juice
& Sluice your pap!

Vamp & munch
– Stomp 'n' crunch,
Do your thing
– Rock & swing

– Let's
Strip the bench,
Hump the lunch

– Pump the park
& Swallow the dark
– Heat the grove
& Eat the stove,
Ready the nerve

– O taste the love!

Sip at the doormat
Guzzle the door
– Gobble the neighbours
& Goose the law

– Season the swamp,
Gorged on desire . . . .

Lap up the bedstead,
Chew the clock
Wallow thy wombhead
Kiss my cock –

  Unbind this mind
Peel my rind
Cook my goose
& Let me loose –

　　*　*　*　*

When your lover
Has gone away
You'll find you're left
With the frying pan –

When you've fallen
Into the fire
  You find you can't
  Get up any higher –

Mating Call 2

for M L

– to you to wit to woo you
gladsome voice like
the lilt and tilting
fluttering of owls
wings upon my eyelids –
fain would i turn within that
flocculent heartbud, heart
curled in heart, breaths
rising   falling   throbbing
as one within our tree
and there bear fruit perennial
unbeknown to mutant man
too deeply twinèd in each other's fleece
for any beast or baron to find out –
yet ready any springing aperture to pierce
to spread our feathers and bare our breasts
and roam the skies and loot the universe
in love that conquers all
outshining every dark night's terrors
– tree of life in whom we dwell
– spell out your secrets
without end, fluttering your
tender soft caress
– owls' wings
upon the eye

from The Journal of a Lovesick Parrot

. . . psychosis
of the living
follows allnight
drunk   recriminations

the raking up
of dying
ember   after
ember, aching cunt
and member

. . . old cat scratching
mutely for admission
at child-guardian's door

husband pleading mutely
gimme   confirmation
early morning fuck
masked in silence
and trembling
not to wake the child

. . . invading dreams
the other side
of thin partitions

or dreaming
of being
invaded

. . . sticky cringing creatures
aching for
the soft machine
the hard stuff
sex and love

to grind our bones
not much to ask

dawn's breath glimmers
over cat and child

cock rears up and crows
into shining mother mild

. . . till clock's drill kills
the call of the wild

takes hope to task
too much to ask

though it seemed so little
only wanting
birth and rebirth

a cuddle   a snuggle
a suck and a fuck

to lose ourselves
to find one
another, our
selves in
each other

. . . so little to ask
so much to give
so hard to take
so tough to live

at peace
with our needs
and desires

when no person
is there
to answer
to fulfil them

nor wants you
to nourish
their own

. . . when the will
to stay open, to touch
and be touched

has died
in the empty-bed
empty   fullness
of time

no peace of mind
no passion spent

only the blues
these letters
not sent

SEA SONG

Lips part   *breaking*
   shored bowstring   *ebbing*
  arrows –   echoes
of violin gut   *flowing*
  to the conductor's
   fingertip command
then snapping
  mouth
   opens   wide   *breaking*
its tongue
  barks –   foams   *ebbing*
  reft of music
   babbles bricks
throat spews   *flowing*
   old newsreels
drunken toasts
  on boats and tides   *breaking*
   high ideals   *ebbing*
with dynasties
  flags   – great quests
   loves and deaths
long forgot
  battle spoils   *flowing*
   banquet dregs   *breaking*
broken teeth
  images –   all   *ebbing*
   dream images
  of listening
   without taste
or purpose   *flowing*

              – see
the singing
    waves   *breaking*
through –   eyes
    closed
        to sound   *ebbing*
on silence –   *flowing*
    echoes –   arrows –   *breaking*
        mind

                    open –

Gnarling Song

The oak is gnarling
oak door and oak tree
oak apple, oak flea – gnarling the song
of oak breeze and far sea
gnarling the long night
that gnarls he to she,
regnarling the bark
of the woodpecker's ark
in the dark – gnarling
even the starlings
two by two in oak hollows
near the squirrels' ski-run
whence the young leap for fun
over field-nested larks
that unpack their wings
and tune up, up up and away, ecstatic to scale
the toploftical light of the world . . . . only
to drop back, for a walkabout

– till the next arrowshot from the Muse
of birdsong lets fly, and they lift off skydancing
way out of sight again . . . . yet in mind
of loud cuckooland's band
in sweet concert at dawn, dappling spontaneous
its tree-burst of beakfiltered fresh airs free
through glades and lanes, softly priming drunk poets
to pick up, score, twine together and publish
the windblown jigsaws
of leaf upon leaf
of the vast lyric-book of the shires
gnarling on – earthbound and immortal

as the dew-silvered banks
of mellifluous streams
at old valley beds
strewn with blankets of fern,
sun-streaked grasses and shadowblent shrubs
and tussocks of moss yellowflecked
with gorse and cowslips and buttercups gleaming
to mirror God's plenty   — immortal the blodge-trails
of cowpats steaming new laid,

                                    soon to gnarl
— they divert would-be mischievous flies
from the horses, who stroll on becalmed
past cow parsley springing
round a mayflower coverlet
cloaking this head
couched deep in oak dreams
wheezing and snoring and snarling: *Oak*
   — *oak oak gnarling oak, you'll*
   gnarl your roots till you croak

— and thereafter —   infusing new trees
                       with gnarled oaken laughter —

IV Homages & Updates

The five poems that follow are reflections, from 1992, on the sites of five English poems of the past:

Elegy Written in a Country Churchyard by Thomas Gray (1750)

Composed Upon Westminster Bridge, September 3, 1802, by William Wordsworth

Dover Beach by Matthew Arnold (1867)

Adlestrop by Edward Thomas (1915)

The Old Vicarage, Grantchester by Rupert Brooke (1912)

STOKE POGES 1992

(In Memoriam Thomas Gray)

The traffic snarls up on the motorway,
Low jet-planes fire sharp shudders through the trees
Where Gray wrote truth – the golfers swing and sway,
Do deals, curse fate, write cheques, before high teas

In Slough. Night falls. Unheard from newtown tower,
Across still graveyards owls bewail the pain
Of a moon unblessed by love's immortal flower,
Just man's brief flag of pride and strife and gain.

COMPOSED UPON WESTMINSTER BRIDGE 1992

(Homage to Wordsworth)

Earth has but little air to breathe
Or greenery to share; battalions of the homeless wear
Their sleeping bags and boxes like a prayer,
But cast-off newsprint's the best they're like to thieve
From this heartless business efficiency display.
Smoke from mighty vehicle exhaust
And cancer snort clogs every ray
Of sun that percolates the coarse
Polluted surface of concrete-shadowed river:
Dear Christ!   this filthy water's
Thick enough to walk on – but all trace of laughter's
Quickly spent, as another bomb scare sets the cops a-quiver.
Wordsworth, thou shouldst be living at this hour
In parliament, to put your grass-roots dawn back into power.

DOVER BEACH 1992

(In Memoriam Matthew Arnold)

The sea's a road tonight
And every night, the cliffs a gaseous chrome,
The harbour's jammed with officials, cars, lorries, coaches
Each with only one thing in mind
– To get away ahead of all the rest.
Don't come to the window – the night air stinks
Of petrol fumes, and you'll be deafened
By the grating roar of engines as they gun
For precedence. Confused alarms of struggle
Swell to a frenzy as ever heavier metalclad
Armies of marketing clank and clash
And grind their gears, blindly rolling
Over Dover – unaware of the beach,
Out of touch with the earth, poisoning the waves,
Burning the sky.
     '. . . *Tomorrow, just you wait*
And see,' went Vera Lynn's song of hope
And Tommy glory – but that old human story's
Dead and long forgotten
Under the sea that's a road tonight
And every night on which nobody waits

Or sees.

NOT ADLESTROP

(Homage to Edward Thomas)

No, I don't remember Adlestrop
(Moreton-in-Marsh's the nearest stop)

But when I was small there were puffer trains
Cresting bridges that wound over leafy lanes

And one that stopped at a long white gate
To let a herd of cows pass, late

One summer evening at a level crossing
In the Cotswold hamlet of Little Bossing.

GRANTCHESTER 1992

(In Memoriam Rupert Brooke)

God*damn*!   to see the vid-freaks whirr
Trampling the graves at Grantchester!
To see dawn bin-bags heaped and smelly,
To hear the blare of pop and telly . . .

To see Lord Archer's stately pile
Past which massed cars and tourists file
– Say, is he within, the fragrant feller
Churning out some crass best-seller?

When the Church clock strikes half-past three
There's take-away and chips for tea
Whilst Brooke's shade, unheard in a chestnut-tree
Shrills   '– *Save England, my England, from the EEC.*'

A Fanfare for Thribb

(Lines occasioned by E. Jarvis Thribb's
first foray into the open arena of
Parnassus In Our Time)

So. E. J. Thribb[1]
You are taking
To the hardbacked
Stage.

Your natural
Modesty overcome
By the call
To communicate

Helping to save
The good, if
Rotting ship Britain
At one of
Her many
Darkest hours.[2]

Not for you
The vulgarity of
Industrial action
Or a closed shop
For verse-mongers.

Your star
Is in the
Ascendant.
Your power will
Not be cut.

[1] E. J. Thribb, the South London bard whose topical and obituary verses, at
once sharply pointed and slyly understated, have appeared in every issue of
Private Eye magazine since 1972. His lines tend to be short to fit into the Eye's
narrow columns. He's a universally acknowledged master of unexpected,
abruptly evocative line breaks.
[2] The publication of Thribb's first collection (see note 6 below) coincided with
a period of particularly demoralised and disruptive industrial unrest across
Blighty.

No doubt, then
Your name and
Unassuming nature
Are soon to be
(Or not to be?
'This', to quote you
On Howard Hughes,
'Is the enigma' . . .)[3]
    – A culture vultures'
Darling, a household
Word

Along with Brillo,
Freud egg and Bacon,
Pete 'n' Dud,
G. Mary Wilson, the dreaded
Pam Ayres, Melvyn Bard,
Lord O'Luvvier, Twiggy
And the Turds.[4]

Thribb's hitherto
More privately
Distilled wit and wisdom
Will be re-
Gurgitated
Like theirs
On the boards
Of music halls –
Across fitted carpets
Of TV parlours
In suburban bar-rooms,

[3] On 16 April 1976 Thribb had written ('In Memoriam Howard Hughes'):
'So. Farewell then/Howard Hughes/Mystery millionaire.//It would seem
that/You are dead//But are you?//We have been/Hoaxed before//So why not
now?/But then. Does/Anyone *really* die?/This is the enigma.'
[4] Spiggy Topes and the Turds were a spoof pop group invented for the Eye by
Peter Cook. Thribb was wont to lament their recordings, TV spots, concerts,
PR ballyhoo and musicianship as 'abysmal'.

Late night Discos, Soup
Kitchens and gutters
With Heavy Sausage[5]
And chips.

Wherefore
Write on, pungent
Elegiac and Occasional
Celebrant and debunker.
Quite possibly
The last
Of the Few
Truely
International Voices,
Who include
Foreign poem-smiths
Such as Omar
Khayyam, Jeremiah
And Muhammad Ali.

So *Ho*! *Olé*, and Hail
But not Farewell.
You'll surely
Fight on
For many a cold winter
From your Corner –
Big-Time bloodied
And perfect
Bound, but unbowed
Incorruptible spokesman
Setting your sights
On the unjustly
Under-exposed

[5] Heavy Sausage was another band created by *Private Eye* writers which, as
well as adding pith to the organ's mockery of the music business, actually
played a lot of jazz gigs around London, including a four-year residency at
Chelsea Arts Club in the late 1970s. It featured Barry Fantoni, Miles Kington,
Chris Welch and other journo-musicians. Thribb's association with these men
did not deter him from writing, with characteristically terse detachment, 'Their
lyrics/Are rubbish frankly'.

Such as Ludwig
Koch, Birdsong Recorder
No less than
The (arguably) great
Masters like Sir Noël
Coward or W.
Somerset Maugham.

Moving on
With the times
But not always
In step.
There you go
(If you'll pardon
The Americanism)
Never pulling
Your punches

Only more pints
And smaller measures
Of the hard stuff
(I know
You don't
Drink. Whereas I
Do indulge
In extra-
Poetic licence. Perhaps
That's why this
Poem is nearly
As long as your
Entire collection)

    – I mean your special
Home-brewed well
Of poetry that stuns
And is still
At the same
Time immediately
Understood

And enjoyed
Served up brimming
Not only
As was ever
Your knack
Into our world-weary
(8 point)
Print-sized
Eyes

But also
Now poised
To enter
Our libraries,
And our descendants'
Exam papers
Even, perhaps.

This elegantly
Produced first book[6]
Is the least you deserve
For so selflessly
Arresting your
Development at 17,
To record for us others
The dialects
Of our island
Tribe

For better,
And for verse,
Always from your
Critically
Cool yet unclouded
Late teenager's
Point of view.

[6] *So. Farewell Then . . . and Other Poems* by E. J. Thribb (17), Elm Tree, London, 1978.

So Voilà, three cheers,
Oyez and Hear Hear
Say I, and here's
Wishing you luck
(You may need it)
In your new career
With this brave
New departure,
The slim vol
League.

It could lead
Directly
Eric, or
Little by little (as
In my own case
Alas)
To a rest-cure
Of vintage
Years on tour

Flowing free,
And drinking free
Too – to be launched
Is usually
To succumb –
In any number
Of switched-on
Real Ale pubs.

Though you may
Prove
Too shy, or un
Swervingly devoted
To the straighter
Side of
The Muse.

Fame
To your credit
Has never been
Your bag,
If you'll bear
With another
Imported coinage
Some of the younger
Pseuds are
Using.

Either way
The universities
And critics who
Had never even
Heard of you
Will know now
Your fortnightly
Workmanship, timeless
Gaze and terrific
Frankness, *Mon
Gervais*, are not
To be sneezed at.

Any more than
The true greats
Dickens (though his
More rhetorical
Poetry was
Serialised
In prose), MacGonerballs,
The True Story-tellers
Logue, Alfred 'itchcock
And Alfred, Lord Tennis-
Person
Or the incumbent
Old lorry-hater
Yon Betjemate.

Strange names
These, for the stable
Mates of poets
With more ordinary
Ones like E. Thomas,
D. Thomas, R. S. Thomas,
D. M. Thomas, Sir Thomas
Wyatt and that too oft
Forgotten old-timer, good
Old Thomas the Rhymer.
Also Michael Smith,
Stevie Smith, and Ben,
Samuel, or Linton
K. Johnson – and
Of course Eliot,
T. S., not to mention
Thribb, E. J.

Although
Come to think of it
I *have* just mentioned
Him. What a misleading
Phrase 'not to mention'
Is.
But such
Are the impossible
S-bends language forces
Us to plumb.

Another
E. J. I probably
Ought not to mention
Is E. J. Hobsbawn the
Historian because
I do not think
He has ever
Aspired
To be a poet.

Whereas
Your restoration
Of plain speech
To the folklore
Of what was once
Perhaps (as Keith
Sometimes thinks) wrongly
An Imperial Nation –
Chronicling
Its myths, commemorating
Its dead, and
Refining the taste
Of the (newly Arab
Owned) Welfare
State –
May one day
Be rewarded
With an old-
Fashioned Knighthood.

After several changes
Of government
Admittedly.
I hope your mum
And Keith's mum
Will still
Be alive.

Not forgetting
Yours truly
– Ironically, yet
Most sincerely (suck suck)
Your fan.
However as
I'm nearly 65 – how time
Flies for the freelance – I
Trust that you'll
Give me a good
Write-up too
Before you too

(Sorry about that)
Slightly jarring note
Of two *too*s
In two lines)
– Retire in turn . . .

    And eventually appear
Alongside Longfellow,
Blake and Big Ted
(To the amazement
Of Keith's kids)
In that most golden
Of treasuries,
The obituary column
Overseen by St Peter
For the transcen-
Dentally Private
Eyes of eternity.

A POSTCARD FROM IRELAND

(sound-poem score for contraction or extension
with improvised or illegible noises)

Homage to Joyce and Schwitters

Behold – out of nowhere – a message
emblazoned

across   the sky:

GUINNESS FOR STRENGTH

. . . Only these words
are (obliquely)
incumbent
upon him –

. . . The compleat angler
is silent
bringing
his catch
of a lifetime
to land:

But the giant fish

a s
  i t g l E A P s

from the stream

g u t - c u r d l e s

H
its death thROEs
T

of the line

from the end

81

'– E e ? e H r r H a – Mmmm . . . What's this ? – Gurrk!

– A sliver? A silver? – A mettel? – A . . . URggh
– 'Tis – a Hook . . . Yass – graach – OI'm hookt . . .

What's this? – Eeeps . . . Gassshhh i' th' gummmn –
Who's that? – A cunning litle man –
                                tinks hisself KINGfisher-
man . . . . . . Yank is ut – on t'other bank –
Oi'll give ya – what for –
                      for what the Hn'GECK
R'yoo . . . yankin' me for? Just a sporting
prank, is ut? A joke?
              – Hawhawhaw
              tray tray droll . . . .

82

– And then, monstrous killer –   you'd have me smoked

Or cooked –   or pummelled to paste

Oi'll be bound –

    . . . and be gutted –   and ground

    . . . on your plate

        – 'Tis an act of   – otter hate

– and yet

    your kind

        will be saying

            the while

                with a smarmy self-

approblOAting smile

        how you just

            . . . *Louvre* the taste

                of freshwater salmon

– Now see heirr, Mister Mammon, just you wait

– willya not . . .   give a jot

    have a care   – EEk . . .

              Why d'ya seek

to drag me out – how can ya dare

exult

  to see me writh*e*

          and twitc*h*

                  – gill-gagged and homeless

     and shou*t*

and thrash

in your   (so-called) upper air –

pulled ——————— – ou t . . . o u t and a w a y

way out   out

from mi own

belov'd

.....s t r e a m

of consciousness

– where I've been wont to

Le^ap _{and} d^art

and flash mi silvers, and freely fart

_avoidin' thi big pikes

_an' spawnin' mi littel mikes

– doin' mi ting

fondlin' wit mi fin

_tinklin' mi scales

an' waggllin' mi tail

— Till now, at the end of your tether I flail

spurrtin' s i ↑ erasms at each t u g   of the nail

at the itch of your mortherous kritt∅rkle loin

pitched from your rum-rod, ruthless to die-sect

the loicks

of me —   filty, rapacious swine [except

this degrades swine]

. . . But my age-old Aquarian irritescence

will outgleam your torturous terror-presence

. . . For oi'll get th' fishmate uni

VERSE entoir

you — to multilaterally

drown

an' desTROY you

to bewoe and betide

without so much as a hearse

to look forward to —

just rubbisht wit your tackle an' bait

— like your rotten post-prandial grease down the loo

Whoooscht awa   — to the sea, little man,

to the sea

86

Our battling up-riverbrown shoals, massed
with ironside greys an' singing steel-blues
will close ranks

as ONE FISH

and –   [auauOOooooorg]

–single-mindedly bedazzle

an' blind an' –   [Ooo –   hü   –ü-ü-ü   –

spkruchl – EirrephGLURP –]

... screw and fillet yOO –   [glurp]

Ur ... yass, our ma- mar- [... arrawa –]

... our martyrs' bones will   [KabbOING]

g- g- gl –

Yass will   GLOAT

[Pfoooo ... ach –

as they choke your vile throat –

eegkreech!   –   p-t-sthnoo]

– but soft, stop

– see, hear how

mi liver's —

all hither an' thither an' —

goinggoing

— an' [aɪɡ] —

– GONGD

... at *this* end
of your line

— 'tis streamed in the firmament

— then what can I
— maister

more, but beg MERsea ...
will you not – have murrcey, just
— imagine ... if it were YOO –

— and *ME* theirr
— would I harpoon an' split

in command
an' mash you to mincemeat, as a treat
to gobble

and next morning excrete — ?
— I would not, not at all

— Oh no, Oi'd let you go, oi'd trow you straight back,
roight off the rack —

Don't ya see – we could drink an' swim an' dance together
any weather – tripplin' an' tipplin' with mutual agility
– replenishin' infinite land/water-wed fertility

[GRAACH –]

– O C'mon   – oi'll mmake it up to ya, oi promise mistre
– oi'm a fellow mortal creature after all, oi'll . . . see ya roight –
C'mo –   YarraOOO

I'm SADalmoned to beGOREagh
– an' undone

Heartless predator . . . .

                    a s   f l i e s   t o   w a n t o n   f i s h
                are   we   to   the   human   dish

            – they swill us with their port

                                                    . . . yprGNash

– oogooroonoshtyblurpski –

– oogorooblarpskibloom – oogooRROO

. . . oogoorooKRIMblooeyslager –

Ah-me woe th'remain of . . .

– who'll tender . . .

– how save . . .

– Get-thee-to-boomtown – RAT

ooGOO – you'll-die-of-FAT –   grapple

. . . . . . bimatoozliGRONK –

. . . brutishly deported

. . . th'spawn of –

. . . W- i l d . . .

– d a d a . . . . . m a m a –

– b a b a –

. . . g r E L P s q – '

Whilst a small brown mongrel gaily jumps

in parody

of its motions

and

– as if *he* were going to eat it, yelps:

'w m g o o f'

V Elegies & Footnotes

Self-Pity, Anti-Poetry – Two Voices

*'feeling is first
who pays any attention
to the syntax of things'*
e e cummings

'What is there in life but youth and beauty'
James Joyce

1 Selfish Apolitical Outburst

In this situation, the absolute
pits
of rejection
or hatred, and
lust for revenge
or fulfilment that's likely
never to come –
only ugliness,
old age, sick
thwarted feeling –
only worse
alienation and lacklove
till it's over, with luck
on deathbed and out,

so

– why *should* I care
what Brecht would have thought
how Trotsky would react
– who really cares
what the official line is
or what the New Statesman or the Guardian
or the union imply

– it's what *I* feel (or
in your case, what *you*
really feel) that matters
to me (or you)
in our uppermost

honest-to-badness
egos,
our palpitating
innermost hearts
or secret dreams
or aching genitalia

– *n'est-ce pas?*

2 Responsible Conscientious Reply

... That's all very well
but who in hell
are you or I
when murder, famine, war
demolish so many a door
– next door
or hundreds,
thousands of
miles away –
so many lives
and ever more deaths –
husband hacked down
on the kitchen table
or press-ganged to witness
the rape of his wife
– small children
bombed from this life
before they've learned
to walk or talk
– what do they care
what we *Feel*

... Feeling is last,
a crass contemptible indulgence
for those who've no time
or money or food –
no health, no home,
no hard reliable lifelines

only real pain
– nothing self-determined
– no ease or safety, ever
to muse on whether to vote
or play, or while away the day
– imprisoned, tortured – no freedom
to sleep, dream, luxuriate in Shakespeare
or sex, wallow bathwater or shrink
with a shrink, or expand
with drugs or without
or choose which wine
or dance, or pay
ANY attention to art, beauty, the
fine points of Upper
                              and lower
case cummings
or where to use ampersand,
let alone to re-
Joyce in the rich
and rare excess, *au
fait* with the cream
of the aesthetic play
of the masters
– that untouchable
excruciatingly
esoteric, O
just so
di*vine*ly
sensitised
syntax
of things . . . . . .

for Modern Man (1914–1964) R I P

(Sparked by the graffito: 1914 – WAR
1939 – WAR
1964 – ?)

*'Mentally he is on all fours . . . And what he fears most – God
pity him – is his own image'*
Henry Miller, *The Time of the Assassins*

*'Humanity must perforce prey on itself
like monsters of the deep'*

King Lear

It's as if we were all
under the sea –
where the fallout of man
still implores
the downfall of manna –

'You don't know you're born' –
the things we used
to laugh at on the radio –

I remember hearing how in the Great War
(that's what they called it)
what was happening was quite clear
to nearly everybody.

In the Spanish war
George Orwell was about to fire
when he saw
his adversary had his pants down –

Seeing his cock – seeing him caught short – how ordinary
how could he but see
how absurd to kill –

You could at least sometimes see what you were doing
see your 'enemy' with your own eyes see
him seeing you –

But, I remember, such
mere human considerations
must needs
be over-
ruled:

Govern-
mental-political
hand-me-down blinkers – ideological
Vows-To-Thee-My-Country
were sufficient to outwit
evidence of the senses –

Patriotism dispenses
with 'the accident of'
human life

– And these days
look, the miracles of science
outwit
themselves:

An enterprising soft-drinks firm invents a carton through which
    'Hey
Fresko! You can *see*
what you're drinking now' –
And understanding of the atom has reached a pitch
where future generations of millions can be exterminated
alongside their descendants
at one fell buzz

– Shrieking *Capital! Commune!*   Let *our* name reign
Gandhi die in vain – Bertrand Russell explain
to Socrates, Pope John
to God –

'*Then kill, kill, kill, kill, kill, kill!*'

'*Howl, howl, howl, howl!*'

– Would you rather die
badly, horribly
con-
    tin
    u
ous-
    ly

– or sever
the system. Say
No. Never.

Blast into oblivion the flags –
Disarm forever
the Eagle-Sickle-Swastika Crown.

    – My forefathers came from Hungary
where Horovitz was a town – a place, they said,
where most people lived outdoors
and died in bed – no hate, no dread –

But my parents – trouble enough, after nine kids they had to
   bear
me – in Germany.
When I was two
the Nazis came –
we had to flee.

For that accident of birth it was . . . Fight the good fight
– You're a Jerry, they said at school, &
– You're a Jew, you go to Shul –

. . . 'Hardpunch Horofist' I became & fought
for that same different me

– not for jolly Germany, not the Chosen race
for daily face to face I saw – each one of us
chosen for the human race
– its myriad individuality

Why fight   – if fight, fight for that – for you
and you and her and he
– fight for all humanity

Not in captivated fear – as moths flit about the light
– as though the atom were the monster
when it's we who have the power
to see – or cloud
the universe

a new flower – every day

. . . if we keep it on a human scale,
combat the darkness loud
– sink the doomboom might of bombers' flight

Unmourned mortality of a mushroom shroud.

Same Old-World-Disorder Blues

    . . . Dull opiates, the technological millennium, famine
All continuing, thriving – with terrorists, pseudo-religious
Fixers and hucksters in vogue, inter-
Nationalist gang wars, unbreakable cupidinous
Chains of death sentence: State eats State, Superstar
Complete Unknown, punks scream for more and beat
Each others' heads in – unaware
Of real wild life and vegetation
Dumb to scream *their* outrage   . . . of literature
Reduced to counter-denunciations, party lines
Conveyor-belts, trade counters. Wised up
Students need their good
Grades, for who survives in the west without self-
Promotion –   Then what society
Is this, predatory jungle, spurning the basis
Of its self-possession – that soldiers and idealists
Fought together, worked apart, under-
Wrote a withdrawal from killing? Yet what else gives now
But a slower demoralising of each neighbour, each
'Friend', if they venture on the other's pitch, what use
Writing for sale, when to be read
For what one is worth
Means the reader gives up buying
The sales conference vision
– *Ever bigger profits* – without which
The untouchable bankruptcy
Of the dead-end process
Pushes
      the pusher
            off the edge
Of the corporation's top
Penthouse balcony
To lie immobile, redundant – peace at last
Alongside the dissolving

Wrappers of The Product
On the pavement –
Splayed out, gutter
Of Babylon.

from dreams of sacrifice
to sacrifice of dreams

. . . my son stood over me as I lay dreaming
a long-handled axe held high – then both his hands
dissolved to a walk back up from moonlit sands
to the little town of our long lost
summertime's sweet song. But these were side-streets
I'd never taken, where squashy gourds and
melons lolled at every doorway, with thousands
of red ants swarming in their mulch. Suddenly
from a noisy tavern jounced a band of revellers
led by an olive-green-bearded calypsonian waving
a guitar. I marvelled at the phosphorescent moss
of his doublet and hose, the shook-foil sheen
of his green skin's glowing. Fresh bay leaves and redhot glow-worms glinted through his rasta ringlets
and his roundelay rang like manna across the cobbles.

When he saw me and called my spirit-name
with a dazzling spray of white-tooth'd laughter
I longed to stay and carouse and dance and hug
the gaggle of friends I half-remembered – till a youth
I'd never known who seemed to hate me
flashed his hungry ferret-face and junky needle
dripping jets of blood – it detonated
like a whale harpoon at my eyes
and I woke up screaming   . . . to hack
the whole scene away from deep inside me
and arise – bereft of it, but free

– or rather, safely back on the treadmill, profit
and loss, girding my coins to compromise some more
up the familiar shady lane of present-day
realities called GoForIt, perchance to deal
with death, miss out on high

interest rates, or make a killing, or a flutter
on the schlock exchange. But to sing,
spread wings and fly – to feel
alive, are freedoms beyond the wildest dreams
afforded by these birdless tower blocks
of enterprise, glitter, chart-topping
guilt-fingered dross . . .

A Kaddish for Frances

Cold October '83
your loved ones gathered here*
to share our grief – a disparate
human herd, envying the sheep
their more closely huddled warmth
on the farther hills

– yet grateful, as wave on wave
of the love your life inspired
beats on continuous, at the outer shore
of our understanding, as we board
again the moon-ark
                    treasure ship
– your indestructible word-hoard
tiding us over till we too
the longest journey go.

Night after night your muse's breath
in the trees and scrubs comes calling,
tugs me away from habit and routine
– owl cries swoop in on reveries
calling back a secret music,
the unfinished symphony
of your life and work
– how it steals upon the senses
stately, flowing, clear – the sabbath of
your poetry's leaves

---

* Orcop Church and Rowlstone Mill, Herefordshire, where the funeral, burial
and wake for Frances Horovitz (1938–1983) took place on 8 October 1983.
Five years later, a memorial service and ceremony were held in the same places,
in which she had often felt a special happiness and peace during her lifetime.
This prayer for her was composed over these years of missing and celebrating
Frances. I first read it aloud at Rowlstone Mill on 8 October 1988, to honour
her memory and continuing presence. The phrases set in italics are quotations
from – in order of their appearance in the piece – Frances's poems 'Dream',
'Bird', 'Walking in Autumn', 'Moon', 'Bird', 'Poem of Absence', 'Glastonbury
Tor', and from a letter she sent me in August 1983.

leaves running under the rain . . .
Sunlight glitters in the empty glade

'The heavy change . . .
Now thou art gone, and never must return'

— Yet shines the grass
and sings, echoing
thoughts of you,
your images and words —
prophecies, prayers, visions
slowly cleanse
this heart of lamenting

— for though every second
window-rattle, moonbeam
rewinds, reminds   — how you were
   torn out of us
          — it brings back also
your purity, uncomplaining
   at the burns and lacerations
     of outrageous fortune
— cosseting no grudge, nor fear
save for those of us
whose growth and love
you'd nurtured.

   You knew with Tagore
'Death does not extinguish the light,
it turns off the lamp
because dawn has come'

— sun glowing amber and gold
on woods and fields,
Palmer-light   — gentle birdsong,
scuffling of pheasant, squirrel, fieldmouse
   . . . your *wren, unseen, churrs alarm*
as we return to the paths and streams
of your Cotswold garden
that so many wild flowers bore.

In this valley you walked
— we walk now
with you in mind: your moon's *thumbprint*
                          on the edge of the sky

as we
leave the bright voices on the edge of the wood
and follow again
the bright fish of memory

— infinity of the garden

playing
    grandmother's footsteps,
        reliving treehugs
            and *stillness*
                at the heart of the dance

. . . our radical innocence
                              regained
when your dream comes true
— so let us be
                all walking in Paradise
                . . . all loving one another.

When our bodies
    are laid to rest

        Our spirits fly
            straight up the sky

We gave to the world
    each other's best

        And gave up wondering
            how the wind

forces
        the candles
                    to pray

i.m. dear old P A L (1922–1985)

A lonely librarian in Hull
Found his life increasingly dull:
   In poems and letters
   He unbound his heart's fetters
And now lit. mobs feed from his skull.

'... The trouble is the English are hung up on Larkin. Larkin was a poet of minute ambitions who carried them out exquisitely. But he really isn't a very important poet and right now he exercises a terrible influence on English poetry because if you admire somebody like that so much it means you're not going to be aiming very high ...'

– Thom Gunn, 1989
(interview transcribed in *Shelf Life*, Faber & Faber, 1994, p. 225)

i.m. Samuel Beckett (1906–1989)

Each day unfolds
the map tracing lines
of apparent function,
feet wearily
reoccupy shoes

– must heft me awash
else worked down
to the ground,
trodden under alive
by other boots

the same
old lines, furrowed
sweat of brow.

   Why waste,
throw up each day
this malleable heap
of human clay
to same old mould?

– Only craps
on the gap
laid bare
by his death

              yet
made bridge
with each breath
at the heart
of his art.

Fugue
for John Cage (1913–1992)

Cage   dead
uncaged   head
flying   ears
soundless   bones

            cage   head
            uncage   dead
            ears   less sound
            fly   in bones

bones   cage
headless   sound
dead   fly
in ears   uncaged

            soundless   bones
            flying   ears
            uncaged   head
            Cage   dead

Two Footnotes on Rhyme

The translator Alan Myers claims that '*marble*' is a word
which has 'no rhyme with any useful application' (Sunday
Times, 23 April 1989). Let him consider more closely,
for starters, the following –

Vainly Marmoreal Rhyme:

Though the typescript of my poem was immaculate as marble
A careless compositor still contrived to garble
It.

Mr Myers also regrets English words which, he alleges,
'have no rhyme at all, like the well-known *orange*'. This
well-known is ill-known, as witness these first summer
dregs from –

La Vie en Orange:

Late May, the palest Briton thrills
to two days' sun, cavorts to swimming pools
and tennis – swills Sangria, or Anj-
ou chilled. Come June, the poor fool's
confined to bed, Haliborange,
Beecham's powder and Vit-C pills.

Being

– a footnote to *Seeming*, by C H Sisson:

'If things seem not to be as once they were
Perhaps they are as once they seemed to be.'

If things are now as once they seemed to be
(Leonardo's flying machine, say, or
Orwell's *1984*) perhaps that only proves
The foresight of great minds: but if, as
Sisson moots, they now
'seem not to be as once they were'
(the Holy City of Jerusalem, say, or
Modernist verse) perhaps
It's the result of blindness
On the part of small minds. And without
Staking any claim to greatness, it does seem
To me that things will always be
Precisely what they are – and seeming
Only seeming. Then again, perhaps
It all depends upon precisely *what*
Things are
Being (or seeming to be)
Discussed. Often when this kind
Of speculation comes up I'm reminded
Of good old Blake's remark, that
'To generalise is to be
an idiot'. And if that itself
is nothing
if not
a generalisation,
Very well then –
So be it.

VI Echoes & Transcriptions

Dream Transcription 1980

... Ran into my old Moral Tutor from Oxford – in the College S. C. R. We drew our pens and crossed them, having fingered the thin silver arrows on the caps with nostalgic appreciation. 'Have a drink' he urged, solemnly decanting the contents of a full inkbottle into my glass. It beaded and bubbled at the brim. I must have eyed its Royal Blue hue somewhat nervously, for '– It's all right dear boy,' he assured me, 'it's guaranteed 99% Washable. Got it in '51 from Smiths' of the Corn. A very good year for Quink.' He watched me quaff it (though God knows it tasted ughy as hell) till only the faintest stain of the dregs was left, with a Solv X-radiant inkling of sanctimonious satisfaction written all over his fat gleaming Permanent Red face. 'Here's to Parker's,' I quipped, invoking not only the bookseller and of course the pen company, but also the pioneer bop saxophonist in order to feel one up – him being obviously too unhip to get this reference. But as if to prove me wrong, he then squirted two jets from his recharged pen down each of his nostrils, snorted down every drop, and emitted a high-pitched whinny – presumably to convey his sense of our complete mutual elevated and tasteful contentment. 'Well, must be going now. Going to Kansas City,' he concluded: 'So sorry that I can't take you'   – and left, with thirty-four more bottles chunkily clinking in the depths of his grimy beige betoggled duffle-coat's humpy hood . . . .

For Leon Bismarck Beiderbecke (1903–1931)

Bix's sound . . .

— so often spoken of
as bell-like

yet if you think of actual bells — how many
sound the least bit
Bix-like?

It must be the perfect
symmetry of form
the very idea of
a bell evokes

. . . the unerringly   measured way
the clear notes   cascade and swell —
erupt, shimmer down   ripple and well
from the bell   of his angelic horn

forever preserving   and extending
its cloudless blue   outlines
imploding   the air

— Bye bye   white bird
whose feather-finger'd breaths
like the plangent   dongs of campanology
caressed, yes   so subtly
drew out   those quicksilver
jewelled rounds   and still movements
unimagined inside
creamy cornet   chop jelly

. . . whose bright flame beat a path
hard as blowtorch through mist
– the way through those precious
few nights, dark and light
you laid bare
   the blushing secret
     heart of each song

   blowing bubbles
   O the colours
   of all the jazz
   youthful ages

    that never die
    blown so high

    – perfect syllables
    of recorded time.

FLYING HOME

(manic crescendo/diminuendo
chant for Lionel Hampton)

HAMP HAMP HAMP
    HAMP HAMP HAMP
HAMP HAMP HAMP
      HAMP HAMP HAMP
    hammeringhammeringhammering
piledriverdrilling—fomenting chips—flailing flying
chips and sparks—flaring mellifluous
fizzles and trails—zig-zagging
through RKO-Radio nights immemorial
sparking body-electric ripples
with each touch of the vibraphone's
electric metallic keys—caressing
keys in heat—unlocking
Hampish religion—jubilee chorales
of quivering slish-bam-klonk—*'Hey Hey Hey . . .*
  —Hey Ba-ba-rebop!'
laid down—arrows arrows
of iceblue chips redhot sparks
flying from mallets
slid quivering rills
across clinkscales of silver stone

  —flash
of flesh
   —of teeth—gleaming
       STALAGMITES
and steaming—stalagtites
      —beaming Stalag LIGHTS
and teeming—*STAGS*—
fleetfoot pulsating through forestfires—antlertrembling
spears of steel—hard and mellow—flickering tender—
hoarse-blurt croaking on behind ahead of driving—
on on *on*
—HAMP!

'Hamp, Hamp, what are you trying to say?'
'Aw, de—yaw, er . . . D : E: and, uh . . . G!—ya,
That's what I'm saying man—'

fast Ribs of vast organs—starting thrumming vibrating
fasterFASTERstars—

                        dripping hot salt blocks into glacierdeltas
—bouncing glass marbles—shattering tiled floors
throwing wine-cellars up blitzed stairwells and lift-shafts
through the volcanic maws of crazy pavements
running wild into rivers of molten moss
and hailstorms of mosaic running amok
with drunken glow-worms and night-scented stock streams
erupting a hive of live turtles running
a mock turtle soup chef through to the boneyard
amidst racing breaking clattering cliffs
—throbbing precipices down galvanised gullies
foaming whirlpools of ultraviolet crescendi
stilled by the wings of soft song and silence
that follow the whomps of high waves crested
with spraybursts of rim-shots and chunder and lightning
struck by vibe-hammerclangs and rolling chord-bangs
on anvils of floating unsplintered agate
that split drum-machines into smithereens that
crack open slits in soup tureens

  —soup oozes out
to freeze on pedestals of flaming tongues
of Hamp and Hampmen allstars shimmering—unisounds
of

   Coleman * Hawkins Ben * Webster Sweets * Edison
Earl * Bostic Chick * Corea Charlie * Christian
   Art * Tatum Milt * Buckner Cozy * Cole Nat King * Cole
Frank * Sinatra Al * Grey Jimmy * Cleveland
   Shadow * Wilson Gigi * Gryce Clifford * Brown
Fats * Navarro Art * Farmer Joe * Newman Clark * Terry
   Quincy * Jones Wes * Montgomery Illinois * Jacquet

Dexter * Gordon Arnett * Cobb Johnny * Griffin
Stan * Getz Dizzy * Gillespie Buddy * de Franco John * Kirby
Milt * Hinton Cat * Anderson Charlie * Shavers
Charlie * Mingus Buddy * Rich Chico * Hamilton
Dinah * Washington Chu * Berry Joe * Williams
Mezz * Mezzrow Barney * Kessel Axel * Zwingenberger too
Benny * Carter Betty * Carter Slide * Hampton

—and * * * you

—with massed saxes and trumpets and trombones riffing
in muted obbligatos and blue-note glissandi
jamming hunched or cupping upward
  scatting and chortling—cooling out—then cooking
    swinging their guts out blowing their tops
    beating their records mashing their chops
    building harmonies
                    —chasing and cutting and wailing
      and streaming in light-brigade unison fuse
      flexing ligaments and armatures of compacted sound
      through kaleidoscopes of rainbows melting—
      perpetually re-forming in mutual dazzlement—
      exultant voices
    swirling fingers
  frenzied feet
unlocked horns—
stomping galloping braying

                    —Hamp! *Hamp!*
  —battering—booming—rocketing
your mirrorcrackling hump-heaving big band herds
of guttural nasal lulling-lyrical squealing
  seething groaning screaming pent up
      and final stampeding neon

—all prisoners and jailers of repression freed
heavy keyrings dangling ever faster and looser
till shaken right off and whooshed to the winds
from the all-consuming avalanching detonated belt

of rhythm-
      atom-
           mathematicking over
causing to squirm—jump—dance on higher
   and *shout*
           —that joyous noise unto creation
the old priests called for

                 —but did they tap
such amity of the rooted spheres
              as lights up
         from your madcap
     pinball bell-tower
   to our blood that springs
after spare ribs shaken
in shim
    sham
      shewobbled fragments?

             Send—   rend—   bend—

and though occasionally
  your city jungle anthems'
    whirling dervish cascades
     of rush-hour breakdown
      and stardust in orbit
     stir
        a buoyant tremor
       of skyhigh
         deep sea-
               s i c   e   s
                   k n   s
  —it's evanesced
         the moment
            you touch
            down home
     so smo*ooo*thly
        landed again
                       d
     —yet flying
                        w a r
        ever   u p

f l y i n g

—your primeval plane

—birdbreaths without end

that keep heaven resounding

beaks' babble

on earth

—and hip-haply

brimful

Hampitudinously

heal.

Sonatina

How well and smartly bourgeois souls are tutored
to bow to the knell of Beethoven's dictates
and yet at times I'd scowl, '– I've *had* it
with old Ludwig':   a child's reaction to the years
of being drummed between the ears that He's
the *Greatest* Greatest.
              Yet these days when
I happen on his loudly thumping highs
and rages, feeling his compulsions stretch and grip
the spine, to make us stop and march and stiffen –
chastened, primed – flex muscles and sing
      . . . when hear repeats
      of those well-remembered clarion calls
that knock at conscience, lave all senses
to – Resurgence! Liberty! Exaltations,
Apotheoses, over and over . . . the old glory
inflames me again;
              and then I remember how
– *Hammer-klavier*ed, spirit-blasted into ecstasies
of race memory, prophecy, revolution – too
often we forget
                    . . . . . . the gentle brook
of caresses opening – the Spring Sonata, the secret
spaces of our lives, now flooded with longing
at nightingale and cuckoo
recalled by clarinet trills, with
                              flute-falls piercing

                              far distances, that stillness
before a storm lets loose
      its dispassionate winds of change
      outside the concert's wall – as if
pre-ordained to wipe out the most precious
                    . . . . . . quiet moments
        in whose fleeting air
the unwritten music of the heart can breathe.

– How then

How I'd like to know
how it all began
how snow   & how
who first made man
woman   *little lamb*
who made you
& what cows moo?
How do you do   gentle reader
& say   can you tell
about Genesis   paradise
limbo & hell   from what
kinetic aviary   to which
hermetic sanctuary   how the word
made flesh   why the sky
how heavenly   bodies got waylaid
in its mesh   why air is fresh?
How Adam's breath was blended
why it ended   in Babel
how the word   was so extended
how it   will end?
How an answer   precedes
the question   how to avoid
getting   with it
indigestion?

But when solutions tumble down
I wonder
what is   the problem
is it the Zeitgeist?
'the outward ceremony
is antichrist'
& The Word
is not heard
& a conspiracy of silence
once broken
can never be mended

& then I stop thinking
winking   & blinking
& realise
there's always more
than meets the eyes –

& I know   I don't know
I'll never
really know
any more   than the Japanese monk
sunk in doubt   whose meditations
only go   to show   'Now
that I'm enlightened
I'm just as miserable
as ever'
So I try with a sigh
to throw my self out
lay by the book
listen   & look
to what things are   like
How High is
a Chinaman!
High brow?
How now
about the one
who said How
all Chinamen
are liars?
How he
was one   how
I'd ask him
how he was   &
how he
might reply

Because –

Backwater Windowscape

. .

. .

. .

I wake
and gradually
apprehend
how the pre-dawn
after-rain
       drips
in a precisely
modulated
        sequence
from ledge
  branch
    and pipe

— slow turning
s p o k e s
of a clock wheel
  ticking wrong
  — these notes
    alternate
  in glistening
  alliance

between space

and silence

– like poetry

– like music

– like rain

        drops

    (from
  no
    where
 we
   know)

cycle

       to
       the
       ground
       . .

      . .

     . .

    . .

   . .

  . .

A Contemplation

(Of High Art, Solemn Music and
Classical Culture; with homage to
T. S. Eliot, R I P)

1 Nocturne

Enveloped by inscrutable exteriors
Many, maybe most of us
Toil and patrol away our days
– Weekdays anyway; but at a certain stage
The routine subsides, and like the frozen contents
Of a painting of people
Melting out of its frame –
Out of the museum, all the way out
Of the laws of mortality
    – Or like the letter taken out, unfolded, delivered
    from its insensate incubation in the system of delivery
    for its personal reception – ready
    to be read in something like
    the spirit it was written,
We slip out of the jungle
Of manipulated street-time lines of purpose
Deadly in their automation (each only adding to
        or cancelling out the last
        in the linear stock-market sum
        that entraps the spirit
        and keeps sealed the letter and
        makes you secretly yearn to be a bum)

– To the glade of stillness that succeeds
The exuberant clash of instruments tuning in
A different air – medley of fragments,
Currents, rills and bridges
Connecting the past
In head and heart, tensed and throbbing
With barely defined expectations
To the touch of these fingertips

Poised like Zen archers' to let
   Go the bow-string dance, caressing
With each stroke swift sketches
Of some mysterious fulfilment – a mystery
Yet shared and understood and even now
                  At hand: – applause
               for the conductor, the soloist
                     and soon
Strikes up the measured progress toward
Ecstasy, exaltation in concert, the one
Union with every other
You –
   Double violins, shimmering treble voices, sprung
      Clusters and crevices, suspense and blest release of
                  Music – enter, consume me
Mendelssohn – Mozart – Tchaikovsky – Dvořák –
Bach apprehended via ancient scraping discs of
Heifetz, Kreisler – stately *Air*
On a G String, stretched taut near to
Breaking-
            point – yet
Gently the cadence streams
Resplendent, sustained – till it
Melts – one   in
                  to   many
                        – like the sun
Dappling leaves through a window
Of concert-hall reflections, bathed in
Lustrous beating intertwine of strings
Sawing at forests of memory, shifting
Branch and mass and space
To views and troves and paths long obscured
But all the more immaculately there
                        – Heart's journeys
Out of sombre primeval shade – hinterlands of old Europe
To the trumpeting New World, and unearthly light
Of worlds unborn –
                  Music that takes a civic dome
   From 1977 in Manchester to –

'magic casements' —   the ruins,
Wells and foaming harpsichord

                                    falls of antiquity —
Deeps of timeless spirit

. . . For all that Artaud cried
'*Shit to the spirit*'
                        — his very cry, his whole
Fractured being itself
Another invocation, a symphony in self-gouged meat
Of sonorous blood-encrusted viol woof distrained
Conjuring the bibles of decomposition of our time — the
Orchestrated cacophonies of Bartók and Hitler, Stalin
    and Shostakovitch — myriad distorted perspectives
    of cracked looking-glasses, the 'broken fingernails
    of dirty hands', the broken promises
    of dirty minds, broken bodies
    of disinherited souls —

                        barb-wire-pinioned mobiles
    of prison clothes and decaying skin, gas chamber
    music of the would-be 'Final
    Solution'
                        — leaving
    the next 'Superpowers'
    righteously avid
    to exploit every after-taste
    and refinement of evil.

    With clinical precision
    the Free World's trained thugs
    and forced-labour camps embalm
    the stench of mass-murder
        — transposed by the Democratic
    collusions of the west
    to take in variations
    and not 'lose face':
                        — as witness
    the lost face
    and limbs

of Japanese generations; witness
the late burgeoning
blossoms of napalm . . .

    Martyrs' ashes – the process
    of compost remains
    a grimly plausible
    premonition of beauty.
New constructs spring up
amid mouldering relics
from smashed altar and trellis
beside vermin and weeds
– grassblades, new flowers
emblazon the slaughter-heap,
new chorales of weeping
and uncensored howls
illuminate gangrene,
succour the death-throes
of the body politic.

2 Ode

    And we are *moved*
  By the accuracy
Of the programme, and
Performance   – isn't that
The main point, to see
Recorded, hear proclaimed
A concentrated vision
Of reality? And naturally (being in terms
  of sound, and not fact
  upon fact, 'in the end') it's not
All bad
  ('– Be glad
  for the song
  has no ending').
                    – Silence plays
Its dispassionate part, whilst

We listen and bend
   to the reeds in the wind
   and the winds in the orchestra's
   tree of life,
   lean our chins on bunched fists –
reminded of sacred exultation
   or the implacable pain
   of innocents dying
   in military hospitals

   – as anyone's pain – a flailing babe
catches our breath, that its
mother might happily die
for its safe berth across
these hapless fates
   – that our pity might help it
   stride the blast . . .

                    Now we're
Pushed forward, now drawn back
– Rocketed to what moons, galaxies, craters –
'Faery lands forlorn'
   – Drawn with tympani and harptwang to join
   the ribald lurching pipers' processional –
   looning spirals of clown and gipsy,
   pied jongleur and goliard
   with timbrel and lute and sackbutt o'erflowing
   spout of the blushful Hippocrene,
   the fluted shell
                    Goddess earthed (off her feet)
in electric tongue-kiss to Pan:
good companions well met on a crumhorn-stomp grail
   – tambourines at the saddle and cowbells clanking
tin cups raised, dripping strong ale
to Hail & Huzzah the kingdom of *Come
Together* – singing word make flesh – bodies mesh
on mad May dawns of cornflower blue-
spattered srawberry fields
and hills alight with jumping rams

– orchards with lambs
where nymphs and shepherds sieze the day –
come away, out to play

– Where does it come from
                              and where to go
– Where *do* they go – the refrain and roundelay?
And where can *we* go when, deep drunk yet wanting more
   – It's over;
   Or we switch
And try to get out from under
The emotions seemingly more intense
Than our so-called real (less musical) lives
– To the extent that we'll interrupt
Lovemaking
                    or arguments about money or poetry
   writing or dinner
   to hold hands and listen
   or refrain from holding hands
   to echo that refrain,
      holding to the sublime the song we feel born for
   catching after its distant wavering strands
   as we did to the circus caravan trail
   that wafted fond dreams of a new life
   over the hill
                     – ancestral yearning
   to wend our way back
   to the clearings in the dark wood,
   the sacrosanct places of childhood
   where brightness stirred evanescent
   as the luminous blue of a particular eggshell
   suddenly glimpsed through treetop tracery –
   a fleeting flash of paradise –
   the sight of those eggs
   in a nest temporarily forsaken
   perhaps by the motherbird of a one-parent family
   . . . Where does it go?
                          – To get food
                                    – to mend the strand

Where all threads loosen, orchestras disband and
Cold creeps back in the auditoriums
Now empty of sound – skies void of sun, forests of green

  – To ice; and
Then again
  To water.

        With any luck
        we take it home with us
        and it doesn't go
        but courses somewhere
        through the veins
        of the leaves of
        our knowledge or hope or growth
        nourishing with its flow –

3 Coda

                                        'So

– What in hell's the *use* of all this being
Moved by Great Art, all this
Straining of the soul if
It only makes decent folks . . . malleable
Blobs of goo –
Doggy tears flooding
All vestiges of efficiency?'

  Tricky Dick said it: '– Stay
away from the arts', he commanded his staff,
'They're Jewish and Left-wing' . . .

  – Did he mean, I wonder (if anything
beyond more expletives
to be deleted) that they undermine
The security of the dis-
United nation status quo?
  '– Like, well . . . Jesus   – just look at those
Goddamm Russkies: Peter Ilich . . . Nureyev
. . . Sometimes if you see them plain

Most all of it – even Beethoven – turns out to resemble a
Plain production number, like   (– the election campaigns?)
Uh – well . . . yeah, the
Whole cultural package
A subversive put-on, a kind of soft soap opera
Rigged by capricious gods
For Commies, kikes,
The birds
                    – and the fairies'

'They
            that dwell
in the hollow hill' . . . ?

– itself a wind instrument
whose air we labour to refresh,
whose pristine clarity we crave
from the narrow chinks in our caverns
of selfhood seen by Blake
– the subterraneous oblivion
Plato pronounced

            . . . till we see more clear:

            Daedalus and Theseus
            pulled a string of light
            to be sure, and
            find their way
                            through
back
            and out again

                            – of the labyrinth
            whose intricate self-enclosed symmetry
we can only guess at
from defused clues that survive, as in a shadow-play
– traces of the original
caves of making: a pitch of perfection
we dig at and savour, fixing our senses

on the long-drawn-out notes
of revered old masters

     – as of living pathfinders,
     almost bound by their aesthetic
     libertarian natures
     to bug the current rulers
     and offend the prevailing
     brutalised public ear.

King Lear, like Nixon, stumbled when he saw;
    For those who follow
  Through their perceptions
Of the vanities, the ways and means
Of the imperial process – Bob Dylan for instance
  – Finger-pointing, croaking

                '. . . even the
President of the United States
Sometimes must have
To stand naked'

– The voice of the bard lives on
At the grass-roots, responding to a more palpable impulse
Than the rarefied escape High Art represents
Within the over-all standardised escape-hatch
Conveyed by the belts of supply&demand.

    When Charles Lamb wrote
Things like '– We *are* Lear'
He could rely on a degree
Of immediate sympathy; today
I can envisage a 'general reader'
– One who's probably never heard of Lamb,
Not even Lamb's 'Tales' (or if he has
Would assume they must be something soppy) –
Reacting irritably, 'Who *is* this We
– The wife and me, are you seriously
Suggesting *we*'re the We
You're rhapsodising on about?'

138

. . . And I suppose it might seem
A con or a cop-out – banking on the old-tyme
Good will of some mythical 'gentle reader'
To 'bear with' this or that poet's
Romantic (ie, subjective) drift; and this admission
Leads in turn to the delicate question
Of responsibility in accusation – of
Crime and Punishment, judgment and guilt.

    – Am I without sin
Who throw stones, get drunk, gobble meat
And have not healed the wounds
Of a single political prisoner
    Nor redressed the lot
Of one motherless child: am I not
Inextricably implicated
In the war-machine
I seek to dismantle –
The modernised Minotaur which demands
Unending human sacrifice?
                    – As wanton boys
            To flies, are *we*
To the victims of wars – *we*
Who ingest culture, at liberty choose
What sport tonight.
                    '*They*' have no choice;
    Here it is, inescapably –
Us (who just fuss)
                    against Them
– Knackered, trapped in the vice
Of slavery and starvation, torture
                            to dust.
    – *They*'d surely be willing
    to 'suspend disbelief' . . .
    could we but free them overnight
    to muse and decide at unthreatened leisure
    between staying home tomorrow or going out
    to the theatre or a concert, at one with our 'We'
            (that separates in the very act
            of comfortably seated identification

        – inactive, inoperative, momentary
        enlargement, strictly '*Not*-to-be-taken-away')
  – or free to chance a movie or some pubs . . .
                 Meanwhile
Their catharses cost them dear.

So to speak of 'Us'
As though I held some right
To speak on behalf of everyone on earth
– Yes, of course it's a presumption.
          And the compact agreements
About a common destiny (not only origins
    but meaningful ends)
That sustained our forbears,
Are dissolved – bombed out
Beyond repair.

    At best, the rays
                    given off from new fusions
  Struggle, and fitfully shine
Athwart the waste-land debris.
                       The long reach of folk-song,
The concert tradition
               or poets in the round
Aspiring to restore community celebrations
Can transform by articulating
An audience's alienation –
Its stated common loneliness, tacitly shared desire
To be reunited forever with that archetypal womb.

  One might think, as each person is born
(Even in this mechanically fragmented age
of police-states, pollution, genetic mutations)
From an actual breathing woman's womb,
Each could still, in theory at least,
Recognise their kinship
With every other human alive

  – But in practice, close fellow-feeling
Is all too rarely acknowledged.

At the evening's finale, after the clapping
And even cheering have quickly died down,
'Social' embarrassment interposes its nets:
Most auditors stand up and avert their faces
Expressly away from their like-minded neighbours'
– Heart's desire buried under the commonplace mask
To confirm that anything redolent of communion
Is better kept quiet, a private affair;
When the curtains come down, it's 'back to reality' –
The reality of another day's grind to prepare –
Predictable, constricted – no room to spare
For Pastorale or Passion or massed Odes to Joy.

As for brotherly love – better save it, brother
     for heavens above . . .

                              just as – sure as hell,
     you may quite well have been moved,
     or pretended – somehow contrived
     to imagine you virtually *were* old man Lear
     for a few hours' traffic
     with the stage of fools

(On which the mind-blown King was goaded
To freak out in the cataclysmic eye of a storm,
Stripping off his emperor clothes,

                              tearing down
All the sham constraints and vestments
Of cupidinous man-made awe – to embrace
A gibbering lord of life brought low
     – yet high – disguised – as a veritable seer,
     'the madman
                    bum
                         and angel beat in Time
     . . . intelligent and shaking with shame,
     rejected yet confessing out the soul' –
Knowing
     'unaccommodated man is no more but such
     a poor, bare, forked animal')

– But for now, outside the whirlwind,
Get thee back to accommodations
That 'raise' us from pity and terror,
The thunderclap animal vision
– To resume the routines that secure us
And insulate away ('for now' anyway)
Its untamed unanswerable indictment

. . . So the conscience that dare not confront it
Gets stuffed down the pillows of dream-lore.
Where we lie the more starkly exposed
In spiritual nakedness, poverty, failure –
Our ill-suppressed complicity in so many wrongs,
Grabbing blindly at roots and estates and cuttings
Which admit of no further cultivation
– Least of all by us:
Marooned on traffic islands, tinned in cars,
Sinking – all but drowning – the occasional respite
From the faint-hearted, speed-crazed, money-wasted vapours
Unenlightened by the certainties and anthems
And repeated errors of yore –

History; the closed book of arcane divinations,
Open-ended nightmare with no known absolution

Only the grace of attempting to awaken –
Clearing ground, sowing seed,
Tending plant, tree and child
To grow up straight despite no defined place
– No guarantee of progress or health or harvest
In a broken aeon
                    I know no way of mending
But this dumb show of words
With no true hope of ending

Quotations

The 'magic casements' are borrowed from Keats's 'Ode to a Nightingale', as are the 'faery lands forlorn' and 'the blushful Hippocrene'. The 'broken fingernails of dirty hands' are from *The Waste Land* (III – 'The Fire Sermon'). It may be worth noting that, whilst my poem pays stylistic respect to Eliot, it parts company from the more reactionary of his ideas about Western civilisation and its (dis-)contents.

I first heard 'Be glad/for the song has no ending' sung by Robin Williamson of The Incredible String Band. 'Stay away from the arts . . . They're Jewish and Left-wing' was one of the authorised Thoughts of ex-President Nixon in 1970. 'They that dwell in the hollow hill' are *The Lordly Ones* of Boughton's opera. 'Even the/President of the United States/Sometimes must have/To stand naked' is from 'It's alright, Ma (I'm Only Bleeding)' on Bob Dylan's *Bringing It All Back Home* album.

The 'madman, bum and angel beat in time . . . rejected yet confessing out the soul', figure at the close of Allen Ginsberg's *Howl*, Part One. And the realisation that 'unaccommodated man is no more but such/a poor, bare, forked animal' occurs to Lear howling toward the climax of his own crack of doom in the storm (*King Lear*, Act III, Scene iv).

143

Afterword:
notes on my work
as a poet, performer
and arts circus ringmaster

I've been described as anarchic – a far-out, free-range or spontaneous bop troubadour. But I'm gratified when auditors or readers see that my innovations are rooted in time-honoured shaping spirits, and my dreams in shared realities. I hope I bring together pre-Renaissance inspirations with contemporary facts, without abusing the essence of either.

My early exposure to the rhythms, musics and reintegrative pressures of being Jewish in the post-Nazi Diaspora inevitably conditioned the nature and techniques of my poetic mission. As the youngest of ten children, of whom my four sisters tended to rebel against the more restrictive or unquestioning mores taken 'as read', by and large, by my brothers, I came to assume the role of outspoken mouthpiece for the idealism of the sisters. This sowed some of the seeds which bore fruit years later, when I started dropping out from my postgraduate research on Blake and Joyce, in favour of fulfilling the less academic implications of the diverse kinds of poetry I'd been writing since childhood – and of performing it along with my peers in writing, singing, music and other arts together. We mounted a transmedial non-conformist arts circus, which travelled all over Britain throughout the decades since 1959. Reviving the word-of-mouth tradition doubtless appealed to the part of me that had been steeped in another style of 'underground' oral convention during my Jewish upbringing.

The public poet-spokesman and the cantor-rabbi stand in a somewhat parallel relation to their following. Allen Ginsberg has declared 'Poet is Priest', invoking Blake's Old Testament-prophetic 'voice of the Bard/Who present, past and future sees'; the basis of spoken poetry remains what Langston Hughes described as 'the common loneliness of the folk song that binds one heart to all the others – and all the others to the one who sings the song'. The wheel is coming full circle these days, bringing the word in its various manifestations closer to its origins in law-making, religion, and musical-dramatic configurations. The classic pattern of call and response joints the bonds of Reader and Congregation – although the resultant dialogue and activities are liable to cut across the prevalent civic and clerical canons.

Responding to my fellow poets and minstrels, and eliciting a voluble response myself from audiences that sprang up around us as spontaneously as we ourselves had sprung, I recalled how so long before, in *dovening* (congregational prayers), I'd sometimes caught more than a whiff of authentic catharsis, the tribal pull, toward the experience of being 'members of one another'. And, for all that it was a harking back, I came to recognise positive aspects of primitive forms, such as communal incantation or even the selfsame foot-stomping outcry against tribal enemies I'd shied away from in my rationalist teens. They functioned, for example, in the manner of wild African tomtoms or of jazz horns in frenzied climactic choruses, to exorcise demons – purging the shared emotions of fear (if not always of pity), affirming solidarity (if not always absolute aesthetic or political unity).

Quite often in the midst of supra-national poetry events I find myself involuntarily imagining *yom tov* (a Jewish festival – literally 'good day'), in the ghettos of Sholom Aleichem and Marc Chagall, or sensing that vaunted continuum that links forefathers and descendants – celebrants all, consigned to harmonise, preach, teach, sing, dance, clap hands, achieving a genuinely popular yet ecstatic communion. Our large-scale happenings and recitals, festivals and *Poetry Olympics* events at venues like London's Royal Albert Hall and Westminster Abbey have in fact seemed positively Biblic to some – and more suggestive of the fall of the Roman Empire to others. As far as most of the poets are concerned, we hold with Blake that 'poetry is religion, religion is politics and politics is brotherhood'; and with Adrian Mitchell, that we 'want poetry to bust down all the walls of its museum-tomb and learn to survive in the corrosive real world. The walls are thick but a thousand Joshuas are on the job'.

The voice of prophecy rarely provides conventional directives. When I'd managed to split away from the chrysalis in which 'the Lord is One' was wound round my brain and arm several times a day, to spread my butterfly wings and discover the imaginative diversity of religious and pagan lore, I was almost stupefied, at first, by the rich stores of nourishment available. But old Jewry continued to inform the imagery that burgeoned from the apparently infinite plantations of reference interpollenating.

Even now my spirit reels daily with rhythms and tunes that ran through my youth: the echoes of ancestral lamentations, from fast-days and evening prayers and Talmudic or Kabbalistic ravings; of signal variations of the liturgy – the portions of the Torah, the Psalms and the Apocrypha that kept Jews in touch from every outpost of exile through the ages; of the light-fantastical trips and melancholy of plangent pipes and timbrels and velveteen viol woof; of Chutzpah and Chelm and seriously crazy jokes, the laughter inseparable from tears in Yiddish humour and play; of exalted Hebraic dirges, chants, and benedictions (*duchening*), reJoyceing and overlapping with the wordsounds of 'Hie'brouw clans' in MacDiarmid's Scotland and Bloom's Dublin – tracking back from Bialik to Yehuda Halevi to the Piyyuth and Ecclesiastes and The Song of Songs to the marvellous mythical range of surreal-real praises in which the mountains skip like rams and the hills like young sheep.